Be Ye Inspired!

Volume II

Dr. C.

clfpublishing.org
909.315.3161

Cover design by Senir Design. Contact info: info@senirdesign.com

ISBN #978-1-945102-77-6
Printed in the United States of America.

Dedication

To all women, everywhere.

Acknowledgements

I acknowledge every trial, every circumstance, every person, every temptation, and every situation I encountered that led me to my knees, crying out to my Heavenly Father. I shed many tears as I sought the Lord's guidance. God is faithful and just. Each learning experience was an opportunity to add another ounce of substance to the woman I am today. Oh, bless His name!

Introduction

The purpose of ***Be Ye Inspired!*** is to provide an opportunity for a daily encounter with God. There are exactly 30 days of scripture and exhortation, one to be read each day of an average month. Make a point to read one per day, then reflect on it. Allow the Holy Spirit to minister to you. You might even want to engage one of your friends in a daily discussion about the day's reading.

Cover image - The cover image was chosen due to the exuberant colors it contains and the beautiful butterfly that does is part within nature by pollinating plants. Each woman is a beautiful butterfly, who began as a caterpillar and went through her own unique process of metamorphosis to get to the point in her life where she is today. As a butterfly, you do not have much time to live. So, make the most of each day, and make your life count.

Day One

"For though I would desire to glory, I shall not be a fool; for I will say the truth: but now I forbear, lest any man should think of me above that which he seeth me to be, or that he heareth of me. And lest I should be exalted above measure through the abundance of the revelations, there was given to me a thorn in the flesh, the messenger of Satan to buffet me, lest I should be exalted above measure. For this thing I besought the Lord thrice, that it might depart from me. And he said unto me, <u>**My grace is sufficient for thee: for my strength is made perfect in weakness.**</u> *Most gladly therefore will I rather glory in my infirmities, that the power of Christ may rest upon me."*
II Corinthians 12:6-9 (KJV)

"[T]hough if I should wish to boast, I would not be a fool, for I would be speaking the truth; but I refrain from it, so that no one may think more of me than he sees in me or hears from me. So to keep me from becoming conceited because of the surpassing greatness of the revelations, a thorn was given me in the flesh, a messenger of Satan to harass me, to keep me from becoming conceited. Three times I pleaded with the Lord about this, that it should leave me. But he said to me, <u>**"My grace is sufficient for you, for my power is made perfect in weakness."**</u> *Therefore I will boast all the more gladly of my weaknesses, so that the power of Christ may rest upon me."*
II Corinthians 12:6-9 (ESV)

Apostle Paul exalts his audience with an important tidbit of wisdom, using himself as an example. Having experienced revelations and visions, afforded to him by Jesus, he had much ammunition with which he could boast as a response to the boasting he is hearing from others. However, he understands boasting is not profitable for his ministry, as the focus would be on him and his exploits rather than on the Lord.

Apostle Paul's objective is to walk honorably in the vocation in which he was called: to save the lost. If he is to be effective in his calling, all vainglory must be put aside.

Operating in ministry while situated in this world system is one of the most difficult things to do- if one does not stay focused on the Lord. For Apostle Paul, he said a messenger of Satan sent a device (a thorn in his side) to buffet him (to distract him and cause his downfall). And, when he went to the Lord and requested relief, the Lord assured him that His grace is sufficient for him.

The true is same for us. When we are confronted with trials in the midst of our ministerial efforts, we should turn to the Lord and take refuge in Him. We must allow Him to restore our resolve and then return to the battlefield. Satan's attempts will only prove successful if we allow them to overtake us. We are more than conquerors through Christ Jesus.

Day Two

"Before I formed you in the womb I knew you,
and before you were born I consecrated you;
I appointed you a prophet to the nations."
Jeremiah 1:5 (KJV)

"I knew you before I formed you in your mother's
womb. Before you were born I set you apart
and appointed you as my prophet to the nations."
Jeremiah 1:5 (NLT)

God is the supreme creator of all earth and all earthly beings. And for everything He created, there was a specific design and a specific purpose.

In this verse, the prophet Jeremiah is being informed of his earthly assignment as a prophet to the nations. Notice how God did not decide after Jeremiah's birth his earthly appointment. No, God said He knew Jeremiah even before He formed him in his mother's womb and that He consecrated him before he was even born.

In the natural realm, teachers, supervisors, and leaders wait to discover a person's talents before appointing him/her for a specific task. That is because

humans are limited in their knowledge. God, on the other hand, as the creator, already knows what gifts, talents and abilities He has placed within each and every one of us. So while one person can operate effectively in a specific area and it may be surprising to those around, it is no surprise to God.

God already knows what we are capable of because He is our creator. When you are wondering where you fit in life and where you can best serve your family, your church, your community, and in your workplace, consult your Creator- God Almighty, the omnipotent, omnipresent, and omniscient one.

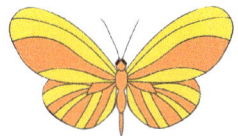

Day Three

"Come and hear, all ye that fear God, and I will declare what he hath done for my soul. I cried unto him with my mouth, and he was extolled with my tongue. If I regard iniquity in my heart, the Lord will not hear me: But verily God hath heard me; <u>he hath attended to the voice of my prayer</u>. Blessed be God, which hath not turned away my prayer, nor his mercy from me."
Psalm 66:16-20 (KJV)

"Come and hear, all you who fear God; let me tell you what he has done for me. I cried out to him with my mouth; his praise was on my tongue. If I had cherished sin in my heart, the Lord would not have listened; <u>but God has surely listened and has heard my prayer</u>. Praise be to God, who has not rejected my prayer or withheld his love from me!"
Psalm 66:16-20 (NIV)

The psalmist calls out to anyone who will listen, beckoning for them to come near to him as he tells of the goodness of God. Specifically, the psalmist wants to declare what God has done for his soul.

First, the psalmist cried aloud unto God with his mouth, not simply with his thoughts. Although it is possible to pray silently with one's thoughts, we can gain far better results if we pray audibly. By praying aloud, the psalmist brought high praises to God.

Next, he states if there were any hidden sin within his heart, the Lord would not have heard him. When we go before the throne of God, we must do so in a pure manner. Therefore, before we petition God for anything, we need to ensure there is no sin upon our countenance. To rid ourselves of any and all sin that would hinder our prayer requests, we must repent and ask for forgiveness.

Third, the psalmist confirms that God did indeed hear him, and as a result, God attended to the psalmist's prayer. Finally, he praises God for not turning a deaf ear to his prayer request and for not withholding His mercy.

As God is not a respecter of persons, He will lend His ear to you and your prayer requests as well. Go to the Lord with all of your desires and make your requests known unto Him. Remember, His grace and His mercy are sufficient for us, each and every day.

Day Four

*"Then will I sprinkle clean water upon you, and ye shall be clean: from all your filthiness, and from all your idols, will I cleanse you. **A new heart also will I give you**, and a new spirit will I put within you: and I will take away the stony heart out of your flesh, and I will give you an heart of flesh."*
Ezekiel 36:25-26 (KJV)

*"I will sprinkle clean water on you, and you shall be clean from all your uncleannesses, and from all your idols I will cleanse you. **And I will give you a new heart**, and a new spirit I will put within you. And I will remove the heart of stone from your flesh and give you a heart of flesh."*
Ezekiel 36:25-26 (ESV)

Even as believers, we have a tendency (many times unconsciously) to idolize our possessions, our mates, our children, and our careers. Idolatry simply means to make something or someone more important than something else. When we elevate anything above God, we make Him secondary in our lives. At that point, we need cleansing. We need restoration. Thankfully, God

said He would clean us and make us anew. He promised to give us a new heart, one that is not cold and hardened by the cares of this world, a heart that has turned to stone. God will replace the stony heart with a heart of flesh. A heart of flesh will allow you to be compassionate, to put things in perspective, and to put your loyalties in the proper order. When you have things in the proper order, you will learn to put God in His proper place in your life, which is first.

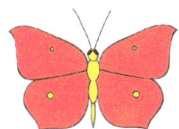

Day Five

"Wherefore, my beloved, as ye have always obeyed, not as in my presence only, but now much more in my absence, work out your own salvation with fear and trembling. For it is God which worketh in you both to will and to do of his good pleasure. Do all things without murmurings and disputings: That ye may be blameless and harmless, the sons of God, without rebuke, in the midst of a crooked and perverse nation, among whom ye shine as lights in the world; Holding forth the word of life; that I may rejoice in the day of Christ, that I have not run in vain, neither laboured in vain."
Philippians 2:12-16 (KJV)

"Therefore, my beloved, as you have always obeyed, not only in my presence, but so much more in my absence, work out your own salvation with fear and trembling. For God is the One working in you, both to will and to do His good pleasure. Do all things without murmuring and disputing, that you may be blameless and harmless, sons of God, without fault, in the midst of a crooked and perverse generation, in which you shine as lights in the world. Hold forth the word of life that I may rejoice on the day of Christ that I have not run in vain or labored in vain."
Philippians 2:12-16 (MEV)

14

In these verses, Apostle Paul was acknowledging the Philippians for their acts of obedience that continued even when he was not present. Think about the service you render. Ask yourself these questions: Do I only serve in the presence of my leaders? Do I serve for recognition in my church or community? Or, do I serve with gladness and continue to do so whether someone asks me or not? Do I serve for earthly glory or to be pleasing unto the Father? We should all check our motives for the reasons we serve.

Wait, there's more. Serving the Lord should not only be in obedience, but it should also be joyous occasions for us, as it is an honor to serve. When we serve, we should do so without murmuring and complaining. We should serve while wearing a smile and having a proper disposition. For as the verses say, we are the light in a perverse world. It is light that drives out darkness. Therefore, let your light (the light of the Lord) shine through you and attract someone who is in darkness to come over to the Lord's side.

Day Six

"*In thee, O LORD, do I put my trust: let me never be put to confusion. Deliver me in thy righteousness, and cause me to escape: incline thine ear unto me, and save me. Be thou my strong habitation, whereunto I may continually resort: thou hast given commandment to save me; for thou art my rock and my fortress.*"
Psalm 71:1-3 (KJV)

"*In you, LORD, I take refuge; let me never be humiliated. Rescue and deliver me, because you are righteous. Turn your ear to me and save me. Be my sheltering refuge where I may go continuously command my deliverance for you are my rock and fortress.*"
Psalm 71:1-3 (ISV)

Family, friends and loved ones are great people to be able to lean on in the time of need. But, who can you count on to be there one hundred percent of the time? Everyone has his/her own life to live and expecting others to drop everything and be there when you need them is a fanciful idea and is just not realistic. The only one we can count on to be there all the time without fail

is God. Others may desire to be there each and every time we desire or need their presence, but the truth of the matter is the load is too much for them to carry, and we should not expect them to any more than they should expect us to carry their load.

The Lord, though, is our help, our way maker, our strong tower. He is our all in all, a very present help in our times of trouble. He will deliver us; He will heal us; He will sustain us; He will rescue us; He will be there when we are heartbroken; He will be there in our times of trouble; He will be there through every trial; He will be there when tribulation finds us; He will be there when the tears run down uncontrollably; He will be there when we need a hand to hold; He will be there when we feel lonely; He will be our protection in the midst of a storm; He will be there when we feel as though the breath has been knocked out of us.

Through whatever we may face during our earthly existence, God will be there for it all! We can put our trust in Him!

Day Seven

*"**But now being made free from sin**, and become servants to God, ye have your fruit unto holiness, and the end everlasting life."*
Romans 6:22 (KJV)

*"**But now you are free from the power of sin** and have become slaves of God. Now you do those things that lead to holiness and result in eternal life."*
Romans 6:22 (NLT)

Christ not only died *for* our sin.. to pay the penalty for sin (which positioned us in Christ and baptized us into His Body), but He also died <u>unto</u> sin, so that the power of sin could be broken in the lives of all who believe in Him for salvation. Not only did the price of sin have to be paid for, as a means of securing our salvation, but also the power of sin in the lives of believers had to be severed - in order to deliver us from the tyranny of sin and its enslaving domination throughout our earthly life.

The first was achieved because Christ identified with our sin so that we might be identified with His righteousness. He died to pay the penalty for our sin.

But the second was achieved because we died in Him. His death became our death, and His resurrected life became our new resurrected life in Christ. It was Jesus' birth into the human race and His sinless life which qualified Him to become the perfect sacrifice for humanities sin. Therefore, He is our kinsman-redeemer.

With His death, gift of salvation, and freeing us from the damnation of sin, we can lead holy lives, which will ultimately result in everlasting life. Also, His righteousness has been imputed unto us, as we have no righteousness of our own. With God's righteousness upon us now and everlasting life a promise for the hereafter, we have all we need in Him.

Day Eight

"Oh how great is thy goodness, which thou hast laid up for them that fear thee; which thou hast wrought for them that trust in thee before the sons of men!"
Psalm 31:19 (KJV)

"You are wonderful, and while everyone watches, you store up blessings for all who honor and trust you."
Psalm 31:19 (CEV)

In this psalm, David takes an opportunity to praise God, eulogizing the goodness, mercy and marvelous loving-kindness of God. David states God has wrought gloriously for His people in the past and has an ample store of mercies laid up for them in the future. His mercies are renewed unto us each and every day. The love God has for us is not demonstrated in private. Instead, His goodness and favor are demonstrated openly for all to take witness of, sons of God as well as sons of men.

Like David, we should utter praises unto God for not only His providence but everything that has extended beyond that in times past, that which exists

for us in the present, and even in expectation of that which lies in store for us in the future.

Like David, we should always have praises upon our lips, for God is worthy of all the praise, glory and honor. He is incredibly kind to us, even when we prove ourselves to be unworthy, for He looks not upon our human countenance to see our faults. He sees us through the eyes of a Savior. Bless His name!

As David says in Psalm 145, verses 3 and 4: *"Great is the LORD and most worthy of praise; his greatness no one can fathom. One generation will commend your works to another; they will tell of your mighty acts."*

Day Nine

"This is my commandment, <u>That ye love one another, as I have loved you.</u> Greater love hath no man than this, that a man lay down his life for his friends. Ye are my friends, if ye do whatsoever I command you."
John 12-14 (KJV)

"My command is this: <u>Love each other as I have loved you.</u> Greater love has no one than this: to lay down one's life for one's friends. You are my friends if you do what I command."
John 12-14 (NIV)

In Hebrews, Chapter 10, Jesus is recorded as saying to the Father that the Father had prepared for Him a body because the blood of bulls and goats could not take away the sin of the world although they were being sacrificed every year on the Day of Atonement. But with the body His Father prepared for Him, Jesus was able to come in the Volume of the Book, the same book that was written about Him and prophesied His coming.

Jesus loved us so much that He was willing to leave Eternity and enter into Time to deliver us from sin and redeem us back to the Father. Can we love one another

to that same magnitude, the way Jesus loves us. Can we?

Can we step outside of ourselves and genuinely love other human beings and see to their needs the way we see to our own needs? You may be wondering how you can love someone that much with all the devilment people engage in. Well, think about this- are you perfect? Are you without fault, without a wrinkle or a blemish? Of course not. And guess what? Jesus still loves all of us, despite our wrongdoings.

He loves us so much that He gave His very life so we could be reconciled back to the Father and be presented blameless before Him. We cannot really fathom that type of love to be shared between humans, but believe it or not, it is possible. Otherwise, Jesus would not have asked us to do it.

Day Ten

"But, beloved, be not ignorant of this one thing, that one day is with the Lord as a thousand years, and a thousand years as one day. The Lord is not slack concerning his promise, as some men count slackness; but is longsuffering to us-ward, not willing that any should perish, but that all should come to repentance."
II Peter 3:8-9 (KJV)

"But do not forget this one thing, dear friends: With the Lord a day is like a thousand years, and a thousand years are like a day. The Lord is not slow in keeping his promise, as some understand slowness. Instead he is patient with you, not wanting anyone to perish, but everyone to come to repentance."
II Peter 3:8-9 (NIV)

When the Lord makes us promises, He will deliver on His Word, for He is not a man that He should lie, and His Word will not return unto Him void. Instead, His Word will accomplish everything for which it has been sent. And it is worth taking note that God's promises will be delivered within His time frame, not in ours.

According to these verses, not only is God patient, but His timing is unlike ours. We measure time in increments of twenty-four hour periods (days), but a day to us could be likened to a thousand years to God and vise versa, for God does not operate in the realm of time. He exists and operates in the realm of eternity.

Mankind, unlike God, is impatient. When we make a request, we want the request to be honored instantly. If it is not, we count it as slack or slothfulness. Unfortunately, in our impatience, we oftentimes miss the blessings God has for us.

We must remember patience is a virtue, and it would do us well to exercise it on a regular basis in an effort to render ourselves pleasing unto the Father. We should always desire to be a sweet-smelling savor unto His nostrils.

Day Eleven

"Behold, God is my salvation; I will trust, and not be afraid: for the LORD JEHOVAH is my strength and my song; he also is become my salvation. Therefore with joy shall ye draw water out of the wells of salvation. And in that day shall ye say, Praise the LORD, call upon his name, declare his doings among the people, make mention that his name is exalted. Sing unto the LORD; for he hath done excellent things: this is known in all the earth."
Isaiah 12:2-5 (KJV)

"Indeed, God is my salvation; I will trust Him and not be afraid, for Yah, the LORD, is my strength and my song. He has become my salvation. You will joyfully draw water from the springs of salvation, and on that day you will say: Give thanks to Yahweh; proclaim His name! Celebrate His works among the peoples. Declare that His name is exalted. Sing to Yahweh, for He has done glorious things. Let this be known throughout the earth."
Isaiah 12:2-5 (HCSB)

The Lord God has been and still is gracious towards us. His mercies are renewed for us each and every day. He is truly worthy of all our praises. We should worship Him with gladness and make His praises known throughout the land.

We should share testimonies of God's goodness, giving others an opportunity to be drawn to Him. God's Word declares, if He is lifted up from the earth, He will draw all men unto Him. He *was* lifted up on Calvary's cross, and He can continued to be lifted up by the words that we speak with our mouths as we share with others about His goodness.

The more we sing God's praises, the more others will want to know who He is. Has God been good to you? Is He worthy of your praises? Will you share the goodness of the Lord with others?

Luke 9:26 and Mark 8:38 say if anyone is ashamed of the Lord Jesus and His words, He, in turn, will be ashamed of us before the Father. Let us honor the Lord today before others by sharing testimonies of His goodness.

Day Twelve

*"Wherefore seeing we also are compassed about with
so great a cloud of witnesses, let us lay aside every
weight, and the sin which doth so easily beset us, and
<u>let us run with patience the race that is set before us</u>,
Looking unto Jesus the author and finisher of our faith;
who for the joy that was set before him endured the
cross, despising the shame, and is set down at
the right hand of the throne of God."*
Hebrews 12:1-2 (KJV)

*"Therefore, since we are surrounded by so great a
cloud of witnesses, let us also lay aside every weight,
and sin which clings so closely, and <u>let us run with
endurance the race that is set before us</u>, looking to
Jesus, the founder and perfecter of our faith, who for
the joy that was set before him endured the cross,
despising the shame, and is seated at the right
hand of the throne of God."*
Hebrews 12:1-2 (ESV)

We have a great crowd of witnesses circled about us
in the heavenlies, cheering us on in our day-to-day
journey. Just as they were able to endure the trials and

tests through which they suffered, we too can make it through the hard times we will undoubtedly endure.

The greatest example we have of someone enduring earthly hardship is Jesus, for He endured the cross, and He did it for our sake. For the sake of the gospel, and in an effort to run the race with the objective of meeting our maker, we must rid ourselves of obstacles that attempt to defeat us.

With the mindset of being victorious, we must lay aside every weight, which are cares and concerns that will drag us down and get us off course. Furthermore, we must free ourselves from the bonds of sin that will weigh on us like heavy chains, keeping us locked down and ensnared by our adversary: Satan. His only objective is to keep us looking in every direction except towards the Father.

If Satan can keep us distracted, he will keep us from running this race with endurance, focus, and dedication. While the journey of life may not be easy, with the assistance of God's Word as our instruction manual, we can make ourselves and our Father in heaven proud.

Day Thirteen

"For whatsoever things were written aforetime were written for our learning, that we through patience and comfort of the scriptures might have hope."
Romans 15:4 (KJV)

"For everything that was written in the past was written for our instruction, so that through endurance and the encouragement of the Scriptures, we might have hope."
Romans 15:4 (BSB)

Here, Apostle Paul informs us of the general use of <u>all</u> the Scriptures, that whatsoever is written, in this verse or any other place in the Bible, is written for our learning and instruction. And, we are to be concerned not only with all the precepts, but with all the promises included within as well. He proceeds to show more particularly the use and benefit of the Holy Scripture, which is, to confirm our hope and assurance of eternal life.

Therefore, the Scriptures are not only written for our present instruction, but for encouraging and establishing

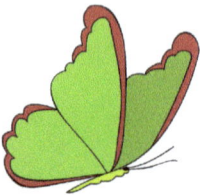

hope of eternal life in another world, under the influence of divine grace because they give us a clear account of eternal life; of the promise of it in Christ; of its being procured by Him and secured in Him, through His blood and righteousness.

Moreover, the Scripture gives an account of the true nature of patience, in bearing all sorts of evils for Christ's sake, of the excellency and usefulness of it; and to strongly exhort unto it upon the best principles and with the best motives. These writings abound with exceeding great and precious promises, and excellent doctrines, big with consolation to the saints; and both serve much to cherish, support, and maintain a hope of eternal happiness; all which prove the divine authority, excellency, and usefulness of the sacred writings, and recommend the reading of them by us, and the hearing of them explained by others.

(Adapted from Matthew Henry's Commentary.)

Day Fourteen

"Know ye not that they which run in a race run all, but one receiveth the prize? So run, that ye may obtain."
I Corinthians 9:24 (KJV)

"Do you not know that in a race all the runners run, but only one receives the prize? Run in such a way as to take the prize."
I Corinthians 9:24 (BSB)

In life, there are a variety of races that people engage in either for sport, adventure, or pure excitement. These races range from relays, marathons, sprints, and hurdles. The one thing each type of race has in common is there is more than one person involved, and each person has the same objective: to win the race.

In order to win the race, each person has to be well equipped for the race (well prepared), stay focused on the goal (do not get sidetracked), stay upbeat and positive (keep yourself encouraged by God's Word), relax (do not become overwhelmed by stress and the challenges of life), start slow and keep a good pace (the race is not given to the swift but the one who endures to

the end.)

Although each person has the intention and desire to win, there is usually only one winner or at least a ranking of winners (first, second, etc. or gold, silver, bronze.) However, in the race that is being described here, each person can when the race of his/her own life.

If he/she follows the guidelines as they are outlined, he/she can win the prize. What is the prize that we are all striving for? The prize of everlasting life, one that comes with an incorruptible crown rather than one that is corruptible and tarnishes by the elements contained in this world system, such as air, wind, rain, chemicals, etc.

Day Fifteen

"Thou therefore endure hardness, as a good soldier of Jesus Christ. No man that warreth entangleth himself with the affairs of this life; that he may please him who hath chosen him to be a soldier. And if a man also strive for masteries, yet is he not crowned, except he strive lawfully."
II Timothy 2:3-5 (KJV)

"Endure suffering along with me, as a good soldier of Christ Jesus. Soldiers don't get tied up in the affairs of civilian life, for then they cannot please the officer who enlisted them. And athletes cannot win the prize unless they follow the rules."
II Timothy 2:3-5 (NLT)

As soldiers on the battlefield, we will endure hardness, as hardness is a by-product of war. When a soldier partakes in a battle, he/she can expect to engage in all possible outcomes: wounds, scars, loss of comrades, and even death.

For a soldier to succeed while in battle, obtaining the desired goal of defeating the enemy, he/she cannot

be distracted by the cares of the world outside of the battlefield. Any distraction could prove detrimental not only to the soldier but to the other soldiers as well.

Also, the soldier must keep in mind that he/she is not there of his/her own accord but is on an important mission designated by the commander-in-chief. In the natural realm (for the U.S.), the commander-in-chief is the United States president. In the spiritual realm, the commander-in-chief is God, the Father. Therefore, as we, as soldiers, engage in spiritual warfare, we follow the instructions and guidelines of God.

What is the intended outcome? To be crowned, with a heavenly reward. To receive the crown, we must attend to God's will and not our own, carrying out His expectations as they have been outlined while at the same time enduring the hardships that will undoubtedly come.

Day Sixteen

*"O God, thou art my God; early will I seek thee: **my soul thirsteth for thee, my flesh longeth for thee** in a dry and thirsty land, where no water is; To see thy power and thy glory, so as I have seen thee in the sanctuary. Because thy lovingkindness is better than life, my lips shall praise thee. Thus will I bless thee while I live: I will lift up my hands in thy name."*
Psalm 63:1-4 (KJV)

*"O God, You are my God; with deepest longing I will seek You; **My soul [my life, my very self] thirsts for You, my flesh longs and sighs for You**, In a dry and weary land where there is no water. So I have gazed upon You in the sanctuary, To see Your power and Your glory. Because Your lovingkindness is better than life, My lips shall praise You. So will I bless You as long as I live; I will lift up my hands in Your name."*
Psalm 63:1-4 (AMP)

Every creature/creation seeks after and desires to have the sustenance within the design of its creation or formation. For example, vehicles specifically operate

with many types of fluids, and one is oil. The oil is necessary for keeping the moving parts lubricated. Without the oil, overtime the parts will discontinue working the way they have been designed and eventually lead to engine failure.

Here's another example: When a baby is born, the baby thrives most when he/she connects with the mother. While in the womb, the baby became accustomed to listening to the mother's heartbeat and voice everyday. On the outside of the womb, the baby will thrive best by remaining in close contact with the mother. Then, to continue to nourish the baby and strengthen the bond between mother and child, the baby should be breastfed, whenever possible. Without the connection to the mother, oftentimes babies fail to thrive at the intended/natural rate.

In the realm of the spirit, there are spiritual beings. Those spiritual beings desire to be close to their creator. In the natural arena, there exists spiritual beings also: humans. Humans have an innate desire to be in constant contact with their creator: God. We long and thirst for the essence of God. Without Him, life is like living in a desert, barren of needed sustenance.

Day Seventeen

"*There is therefore now no condemnation to them which are in Christ Jesus*, who walk not after the flesh, but after the Spirit. For the law of the Spirit of life in Christ Jesus hath made me free from the law of sin and death.*"*
Romans 8:1-2 (KJV)

"*Therefore, there is now no condemnation for those who are in Christ Jesus*, because through Christ Jesus the law of the Spirit who gives life has set you free from the law of sin and death.*"*
Romans 8:1-2 (NIV)

Condemnation, the present and final judgment of God loomed over the sinner, was removed by the intervention of Christ and by the union of the believer with Him. By that union, the power and empire of sin were thrown off and destroyed. Now, the Christian is entirely free from the law of sin and death and from the condemnation that corresponds with it. This freedom for the believer proceeds from the indwelling Spirit and is a direct result of the intervention of Christ that put an end to the struggle waged within the soul.

By "condemning" the law of sin, Christ *removed* "condemnation" from the sinner, those who are not governed, as to their dispositions and actions, by those appetites which have their seat in the flesh, or by worldly views and interests, or by the dictates and motions of the natural corruption, which in some degree may yet remain in them. But, they who walk after the Spirit of God are not only habitually governed by reason and conscience, and enlightened and renewed by God's Spirit, but also follow and operate in the grace and bring forth the fruits of that Spirit.

Day Eighteen

"For the grace of God that bringeth salvation hath appeared to all men, Teaching us that, denying ungodliness and worldly lusts, we should live soberly, righteously, and godly, in this present world."
Titus 2:11-12 (KJV)

"For the grace of God has appeared, bringing salvation to all people, instructing us to deny ungodliness and worldly desires and to live sensibly, righteously, and in a godly manner in the present age."
Titus 2:11-12 (NASB)

The grace that God has afforded us is all sufficient. Not only is it God's unmerited favor (favor that He affords us without us being worthy of it), but His grace also strengthens us and sustains us when we do not have the natural strength to sustain ourselves. Within God's strengthening grace, we are able to abstain from engaging in ungodly activities and worldly lusts. Being engrossed in a world full of sin that we could easily engage in at any given moment, making us prey for the

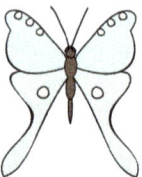

enemy, is not an impossibility, even for the most faithful of believers.

In the power of His might, we are able to abide in His grace and resist the snares, tricks, schemes of the enemy. When we are able to resist unrighteous living, we are able to live responsibly, soberly and sensibly in a manner that is pleasing to God. At the same time, we will be living examples of a Christ-impacted life.

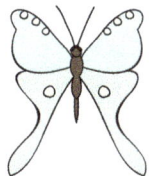

Day Nineteen

*"Till we all come in the unity of the faith, and of the knowledge of the Son of God, <u>**unto a perfect man, unto the measure of the stature of the fulness of Christ: That we henceforth be no more children, tossed to and fro, and carried about with every wind of doctrine**</u>, by the sleight of men, and cunning craftiness, whereby they lie in wait to deceive; But speaking the truth in love, may grow up into him in all things, which is the head, even Christ."*
Ephesians 4:13-15 (KJV)

*"[U]ntil we all attain to the unity of the faith and of the knowledge of the Son of God, <u>**to mature manhood, to the measure of the stature of the fullness of Christ, so that we may no longer be children, tossed to and fro by the waves and carried about by every wind of doctrine**</u>, by human cunning, by craftiness in deceitful schemes. Rather, speaking the truth in love, we are to grow up in every way into him who is the head, into Christ."*
Ephesians 4:13-15 (ESV)

Naturally, as humans, our lives begin in infancy, and each year, we grow physically, emotionally, and mentally.

Every year of life we live can be seen upon our physical countenance. There are many life lessons to be learned, and the behavior we demonstrate and decisions we execute all stem from the growth we have sustained as we matured.

As human beings whose core is the spirit, we must strive to initiate and nurture growth within our core. This growth is necessitated by the need to reach full maturity, so we can be rooted and grounded in the precepts of our Creator. Attaining His precepts within our core will allow us to become steadfast and unmovable as we abound in His grace.

Furthermore, being rooted and grounded in Him will prevent us from falling victim to faulty doctrines that will attempt to circumvent a strong foundation in God's Word.

Day Twenty

"But this I say, <u>He which soweth sparingly shall reap also sparingly; and he which soweth bountifully shall reap also bountifull</u>y. Every man according as he purposeth in his heart, so let him give; not grudgingly, or of necessity: for God loveth a cheerful giver."
II Corinthians 9:6-7 (KJV)

"The point is this: <u>whoever sows sparingly will also reap sparingly, and whoever sows bountifully will also reap bountifully</u>. Each one must give as he has decided in his heart, not reluctantly or under compulsion, for God loves a cheerful giver."
II Corinthians 9:6-7 (ESV)

As believers, who are equipped with the knowledge of the Word of God and the understanding that we are the adopted sons of God and co-heirs with Jesus, we expect His best in all areas of our lives because that is what His Word promises us. And as such, we have learned to tap into the promises that have been afforded every believer.

One of those promises is embedded in this verse: If we

sow bountifully, we will reap bountifully. What's really important about this principle is it is applicable across the board. For example, if you give bountifully in finances, you will be blessed bountifully in finances. If you give love to others abundantly, others will love you abundantly. If you give amply of your time to the work of the kingdom, time for your own affairs will be provided.

Conversely, there is another principle that mirrors this one with the opposite effect. If we sow sparingly, we will reap sparingly. So, the question you should ask yourself is: How do you want to receive from God, bountifully or sparingly?

Day Twenty-One

"But let him ask in faith, nothing wavering. For he that wavereth is like a wave of the sea driven with the wind and tossed. For let not that man think that he shall receive any thing of the Lord. <u>A double minded man is unstable in all his ways</u>."
James 1:6-8 (KJV)

"But when you ask him, be sure that your faith is in God alone. Do not waver, for a person with divided loyalty is as unsettled as a wave of the sea that is blown and tossed by the wind. Such people should not expect to receive anything from the Lord. <u>Their loyalty is divided between God and the world, and they are unstable in everything they do</u>."
James 1:6-8 (NLT)

In these verses, James is clear that a person's intentions and loyalty should be without wavering. This sentiment is mimicked by John in Revelation 3:16 (NKJV) when he says, *"So then, because you are lukewarm, and neither cold nor hot, I will vomit you out of My mouth."* God requires of those who say they are His to be completely

dedicated to Him.

Those who are unsure of where they stand with God or with the world should quickly decide where they <u>will</u> stand. Otherwise, they will stand in rejection from God as a result of their instability. God will not settle for being second best nor will He contend with someone's divided loyalty.

In Exodus 34:14 (NASB), it states, *"for you shall not worship any other god, because the LORD, whose name is Jealous, is a jealous God."* God is sure about His expectations of us, and we should be equally sure about our loyalty to Him. We should willingly declare with gladness, *"If we live, we live for the Lord; and if we die, we die for the Lord. So, whether we live or die, we belong to the Lord"* Romans 14:8 (NIV).

Day Twenty-Two

*"Make a joyful noise unto the LORD, all ye lands. Serve the LORD with gladness: come before his presence with singing. **Know ye that the LORD he is God: it is he that hath made us, and not we ourselves; we are his people, and the sheep of his pasture.** Enter into his gates with thanksgiving, and into his courts with praise: be thankful unto him, and bless his name. For the LORD is good; his mercy is everlasting; and his truth endureth to all generations."*
Psalm 100:1-5 (KJV)

*"Shout to the LORD all the earth! Serve the LORD with joy. Come before him with a joyful shout! **Acknowledge that the LORD is God. He made us and we belong to him; we are his people and the sheep of his pasture.** Enter his gates with thanksgiving and his courts with praise. Thank him and bless his name, for the LORD is good and his gracious love stands forever. His faithfulness remains from generation to generation."*
Psalm 100:1-5 (ISV)

As believers, we are God's sheep, and we graze in His pasture. He gave us life, causing us to exist. He formed our bodies and is the Father of our spirits. We did not and we could not make ourselves. Therefore, we are not our own, but we are His. He has an incontestable right to us and all things. We are His and we function by His power, disposed of by His will, and are devoted to His honor and glory.

God is our sovereign ruler. He gives law to us as moral agents and will call us to an account for everything we do. As believers, we are not at liberty to do what we will, but we must always make conscience of doing as we are bidden.

God is our bountiful benefactor. We are not only His sheep, whom He is entitled to, but we are the sheep of His pasture, of whom He gives great care. The One who made us maintains us and gives us all good things to richly enjoy.

Day Twenty-Three

"And Jesus said unto them, Because of your unbelief:
for verily I say unto you, If ye have faith as a grain of
mustard seed, ye shall say unto this mountain, Remove
hence to yonder place; and it shall remove; and
nothing shall be impossible unto you."
Matthew 17:20 (KJV)

"He said to them, 'Because of your little faith. For
truly, I say to you, if you have faith like a grain of
mustard seed, you will say to this mountain,
"Move from here to there," and it will move,
and nothing will be impossible for you'."
Matthew 17:20 (ESV)

The mustard seed is the smallest of all seeds, but it produces the largest of all herbs. Having that information can be used for one's enlightenment of Jesus' statement. In the given context, we could take His statement to mean if we have the smallest amount of genuine faith, we would be empowered to do all things. So, in comparing one's faith to a mustard seed, we understand Jesus to be informing us that if we have increasing, expanding, and

enlarged faith that grows and is strengthened from small beginnings, we can perform the most difficult undertakings.

The principle of vitality is exemplified in the grain of seed stretching forward to great results. The same principle is thus illustrated in the nature of faith. Our faith should be like that.

Possessing that type of faith affords us the authority to speak to our situation and command it to change. To illustrate that principle, Jesus probably pointed to a nearby mountain to assure the disciples that if they had that level of faith, they might accomplish the most difficult undertakings, even those things that at first appear impossible and insurmountable..

Day Twenty-Four

"Can a woman forget her sucking child, that she should not have compassion on the son of her womb? yea, they may forget, yet will I not forget thee."
Isaiah 49:15 (KJV)

"Can a woman forget her nursing child And have no compassion on the son of her womb? Even these may forget, but I will not forget you."
Isaiah 49:15 (NASB)

Be assured that God has a tender affection for His church and people, despite their flaws, misgivings, tendencies, or shortcomings. Regardless of the circumstances they may face, God would never desire for them to be discouraged when seeking a solution to the challenges they face or when they make a wrong turn during a trial.

Reading this verse about the possibility of a mother forgetting the child she nursed may cause sadness. But, unfortunately, it is an unfathomable reality. While most mothers are natural nurturers, other mothers do neglect their children. In contrast, the compassion God holds for

His people infinitely exceeds that of the tenderest parents toward their children, the parents who will risk life and limb for them.

Imagine that for a moment, parents who would put themselves in harm's way to protect their child. Imagine the amount of love the parents have that flows from their heart, the love that protects to the best of their ability.

Imagine that love multiplied to an inifinite degree. That is how much God loves His people. His love is immeasurable. With God's love comes His promise: to never leave us or forsake us. He will be with us throughout eternity.

Day Twenty-Five

"For I am persuaded, that neither death, nor life, nor angels, nor principalities, nor powers, nor things present, nor things to come, Nor height, nor depth, nor any other creature, shall be able to separate us from the love of God, which is in Christ Jesus our Lord."*
Romans 8:38-39 (KJV)

"For I am sure that neither death nor life, nor angels nor rulers, nor things present nor things to come, nor powers, nor height nor depth, nor anything else in all creation, will be able to separate us from the love of God in Christ Jesus our Lord."*
Romans 8:38-39 (ESV)

In Christ, we have security. By the action of His death, He paid our debt. Therefore, divine justice was satisfied. Then, upon His ascension, we have an advocate at the right hand of God; all power is given to Him. He is there, making intercession. As a believer, our soul says within us, "He is mine, and I am His! And, we long to please Him and live with Him!"

That desire enables our belief in Him, He who justifies the ungodly. It was all a part of God's plan for our redemption. God manifested His love for us by giving His own Son. Is there any reason why He should turn aside or do away that love?

Nothing can take Christ from the believer, and nothing can take the believer from Him. Is there anyone or anything you can say the same about? No. And, there will come a time when we must depart this earth, for we must all die as that time is appointed unto man. But the soul that is in Christ, when other things are pulled away, cleaves to Christ. When death comes, all bonds of other unions are broken, even that of the soul and the body. The believer's soul will be unified with the Lord Jesus and will enjoy Him forever. How beautiful that union will be.

Day Twenty-Six

*"Fear thou not; for I am with thee: be not dismayed;
for I am thy God: **I will strengthen thee; yea, I
will help thee;** yea, I will uphold thee with the
right hand of my righteousness."*
Isaiah 41:10 (KJV)

*"Do not fear, for I am with you; do not be afraid,
for I am your God. **I will strengthen you; I will
surely help you;** I will uphold you with My
right hand of righteousness."*
Isaiah 41:10 (BSB)

In this verse, God is giving us, His children, assurance that no matter what we may endure throughout our earth's journey, He will be with us through it all. He cautions us about walking in fear and anxiety and allowing the cares of the world to wear us down. People only need to fear or be anxious when they lack an adequate support system. God is the only support system we need, and although we may grow weary, we will not suffer defeat, for He is our ever-present help in our times of need. He will not only strengthen us, but He will provide help.

Take a moment and look back over your life. Review the challenges you faced in the past. Do you recall God being with you? Do you recall Him providing assistance for you? Do you recall Him giving you much-needed wisdom, counsel, and answers? Has He given you a reason to think that would change? Or, that He would cease being your all in all, your way maker, your strong tower, your place of refuge, your peace, your hedge of protection, or the bright morning star?

Remember, God is the same as He was yesterday. He is that same god today, and He will be the same god forever more. Therefore, it is safe to place your complete trust in Him.

Day Twenty-Seven

"If my people, which are called by my name, shall humble themselves, and pray, and seek my face, and turn from their wicked ways; then will I hear from heaven, and will forgive their sin, and will heal their land."
II Chronicles 7:14 (KJV)

"If my own people will humbly pray and turn back to me and stop sinning, then I will answer them from heaven. I will forgive them and make their land fertile once again."
II Chronicles 7:14 (CEV)

As humans, we sometimes have a tendency to seek the hand of God and His favor while living anyway we choose. And even when our choices do not line up with God's Word, yet and still, we have the expectation that He will honor us regardless of our behavior and our disobedience. This verse tells us clearly that the Lord has expectations of us, and when we adhere to His expectations, He will withhold no good thing from us.

Our relationship with the Lord is a two-way street. God expects that His people who are called by His name, if they have dishonored His name by their iniquity, should

honor it by accepting the punishment of their iniquity.

The key though is not to serve for the benefit of rewards, but to serve with a servant's heart, one that is fully dedicated to see the work of the kingdom carried out: the saving of lost souls. Our job on earth is to spread the gospel of the Good News of Jesus Christ, which is His death, burial, and resurrection. It is our job to point people toward heaven, to point people toward God. If we do that and make that our singular focus, we will have a great reward in heaven.

We must humble ourselves under His hand, must pray for the removal of the judgment, must seek His face finding the favor of God; and yet all this will not do unless we turn from our wicked ways and return to the God from whom we have revolted.

God expects us, as His children, to submit ourselves humbly before Him. He expects us to be in constant communication with Him through the vehicle of prayer. He expects us to not walk in the ways of sin, transgressing against Him. When we adhere to the expectations of the Lord, then we can expect Him to answer our pleas and requests in return.

Day Twenty-Eight

"And he said unto me, My grace is sufficient for thee: for my strength is made perfect in weakness. Most gladly therefore will I rather glory in my infirmities, that the power of Christ may rest upon me. Therefore I take pleasure in infirmities, in reproaches, in necessities, in persecutions, in distresses for Christ's sake: for when I am weak, then am I strong."
II Corinthians 12:9-10 (KJV)

"And he hath said unto me, My grace is sufficient for thee: for my power is made perfect in weakness. Most gladly therefore will I rather glory in my weaknesses, that the power of Christ may rest upon me. Wherefore I take pleasure in weaknesses, in injuries, in necessities, in persecutions, in distresses, for Christ's sake: for when I am weak, then am I strong."
II Corinthians 12:9-10 (ERV)

It is human nature to avoid challenges. We avoid them because we do not know if we are fully equipped to handle them emotionally, educationally, physically, financially, or spiritually. Rather than fail at a challenge, it is easier to try to escape it all together.

Furthermore, in the midst of a challenge, our human bodies can become fatigued, overwhelmed, withdrawn, fearful, stressed, or filled with anxiety. However, in our human weakness and deficiency, we can take pleasure in knowing we do not have to rely upon our own strength. All we need to function effectively is to operate in the strengthening grace of God instead of attempting to rely upon our human strength, knowledge and abilities.

God's strengthening grace allows us the ability to face challenges head on instead of running from them in an attempt to avoid the inevitable. In Him, trials can become non-factors in our lives, as God's grace will prevail as it strengthens us for the trials. So, instead of resisting what lies ahead, we should embrace the challenge and go through it, knowing God's grace will sustain us because His grace is sufficient for us. In Him, we live, we move, and we have our being. Thus, we will have the endurance needed to make it through each and every trial.

Day Twenty-Nine

*"<u>Thou shalt guide me with thy counsel, and afterward</u>
<u>receive me to glory. Whom have I in heaven but thee?</u>
<u>and there is none upon earth that I desire beside thee</u>.
My flesh and my heart faileth: but God is the strength
of my heart, and my portion for ever."*
Psalm 73:24-26 (KJV)

*"<u>You guide me with your counsel, and afterward</u>
<u>you will take me into glory. Whom have I in heaven</u>
<u>but you? And earth has nothing I desire besides</u>
<u>you.</u> My flesh and my heart may fail, but God is
the strength of my heart and my portion forever."*
Psalm 73:24-26 (KJV)

The psalmist claims his everlasting devotion to God, the one who guides him with His counsel and will do so each and every day of his earthly existence. The psalmist vows to lean not to his own understanding but to depend on God's guidance.

The psalmist acknowledges that his heart may fail him, knowing it is deceitful and wicked (Jeremiah 17:9). And,

to make matters worse, his flesh may fail him. Psalm 23:7 says, *"For as he thinketh in his heart, so is he: Eat and drink, saith he to thee; but his heart is not with thee."* Whatever is in our heart will be manifested in our flesh.

However, when we set our affections on things above and beyond this worldly sphere, we will have better results in our lives. *"For where your treasure is, there will your heart be also,"* Matthew 6:21.

Day Thirty

"*And that ye study to be quiet, and to do your own business*, and to work with your own hands, as we commanded you; That ye may walk honestly toward them that are without, and that ye may have lack of nothing.*"
I Thessalonians 4:11-12 (KJV)

"*[A]nd to make it your ambition to lead a quiet life: You should mind your own business and work with your hands*, just as we told you, so that your daily life may win the respect of outsiders and so that you will not be dependent on anybody.*"
I Thessalonians 4:11-12 (NIV)

There are many meanings imbedded in making it one's priority to lead a quiet life. The first meaning refers to a life that focuses on your own affairs and quietly staying out of others' affairs. Secondly, it means practicing being quiet to hear God's voice instead of your own. Thirdly, it means being still and quiet to provide time to reflect on your own life, the choices you have made, and where your life is going from this point forward.

In total, living a quiet existence means the greater concerns of the world and your God-given plight are your focus instead of meddling in affairs that are of no concern to you. A quiet life is a focused life, one that focuses on what is important rather than a life of folly. A focused lifestyle breeds respect from onlookers and from those with whom you engage.

Additionally, we receive the promise of not being independent on anyone. The gift of independence comes from putting your hands to working your own business. One that God has afforded you and from which you will reap the fruit thereof. Working to create your own personal wealth affords you the freedom of not relying on others. Your reliance then is only upon the Lord.

Gift of Salvation for Non-Believers

"For all have sinned, and come short of the glory of God." (Romans 3:23)

This section was written especially for non-believers, those who have not accepted the gift of salvation. The gift of salvation saves souls from eternal damnation and is a free gift offered by God Himself.

John 3:16-18 says, *"For God so loved the world, that he gave his only begotten Son, that whosoever believeth in him should not perish, but have everlasting life. For God sent not his Son into the world to condemn the world; but that the world through him might be saved. He that believeth on him is not condemned: but he that believeth not is condemned already, because he hath not believed in the name of the only begotten Son of God."*

This section of scripture tells us God's purpose for giving His son Jesus to the world. The world was in a bad condition. The world was overwrought with sin; the people were living for fleshly desires rather than for God's desires.

As a result of the world's conditions, God decided He would offer the perfect sacrifice that would save the world from being a place where people were lost and had no hope. He decided His own son could stand in proxy for the sin-filled world, taking all sin upon Himself.

So Jesus came, born of a virgin, to save this dying world. He walked on this earth for 33 ½ years, doing the work of His Heavenly Father. At the appointed time, He died by way of crucifixion upon a cross at Calvary, on Golgotha's hill. He shed His blood and died for you and for me. Because His blood was pure, it paid the penalty for all unrighteousness and gave those who believe in Him direct access to His father's throne.

Scripture tells us in Matthew 27:51 that the veil of the temple was ripped in two from top to bottom, at the moment that Jesus' spirit left His body. As a result of the veil's removal, we are no longer required to have a high priest make intercession for us. We, as the children of the Most High God, are able to approach the throne of God for ourselves, and Jesus sits on the right hand of the Father making intercession for us.

But what is even more miraculous than God offering His own son as the perfect sacrifice was the fact that when Jesus was placed in grave clothes and placed in a tomb, He only remained there until the third day. God would not have it that His son would remain in the heart of the earth forever. In order for people to believe in the awesome power of God and His dear son Jesus, a miracle had to be performed. So, on the third day, after Jesus died on the cross, He was resurrected, demonstrating the omnipotence of God.

This very act was the act that would cause people to believe in a god that reigns supreme and holds the power of the universe in His very hands, a god that could save them from themselves.

Today, if you are an unbeliever, you can change your destiny. You can change where you will spend your eternity. Our Heavenly Father gives us the freedom of choice about how we want to live our life here on earth and how we want to spend eternity. In Deuteronomy 30:19, God boldly declares, "*I call heaven and earth to record this day against you, that I have set before you life and death, blessing and cursing: therefore choose life, that both thou and thy seed may live.*"

So, dear friend what choice will you make today? Will you spend your eternity with the Creator or will you suffer Hell's eternal flames? Again, the choice is yours. Just as the men aboard the ship who were with Jonah became believers, you too can make a choice to accept the only one and true living God as your god.

If after reading the above passages, you have decided that you want to spend your eternity in Heaven with God, the creator, and His son Jesus, and the Holy Spirit, read through what has affectionately come to be known as the Roman's Road. This is the road to salvation. As you read through the scriptures that comprise the Roman's Road, you will also read the explanation for each scripture, so you will have clarity about what you are reading and confessing.

The Roman's Road to Salvation

The road to salvation begins with Romans 3:23 which declares, "*For all have sinned, and come short of the glory of God.*" This scripture explains that everyone has come short of God's glory and needs redemption. Then, Romans 6:23a states, "*For the wages of sin is death.*" Here, we learn that the consequence of living a life of sin is death. Everyone will experience physical death as a result of the sin committed in the garden of Eden, but those who commit themselves to a life of sin will suffer eternal damnation in the lake of fire (Rev. 19). Continue with the rest of verse 6:23 that says, "*but the gift of God is eternal life through Jesus Christ our Lord.*" There is an alternative to suffering eternal damnation. We can accept the gift of salvation by accepting Jesus as our personal Lord and Savior. Then, Romans 5:8 says, "*But God commendeth his love toward us, in that, while we were yet sinners, Christ died for us.*" We are able to receive the gift of salvation because Christ came to earth and shed His blood for us on the cross.

Continue to Romans 10: 9-10 which says, "*That if thou shalt confess with thy mouth the Lord Jesus, and shalt believe in thine heart that God hath raised him from the dead, thou shalt be saved. For with the heart man believeth unto righteousness; and with the mouth confession is made unto salvation.*" If we confess with our mouths that Jesus is the son of God, that He came and died for our sins, and that God raised Him from the dead, we will receive salvation.

Finish with Romans 10:13, which states, *"For whosoever shall call upon the name of the Lord shall be saved."* Call upon the name of God by saying these words, **"Lord Jesus, come into my heart and save me, Lord. I believe that you are the Son of God who came and died on the cross for my sins. I believe that you rose from the grave. I also believe that you now sit in heaven on the right side of the Father, making intercession for me. I accept you as my Lord and my Savior."**

Now that you have confessed with your mouth that Jesus is the son of God and that He died for our sins and rose from the grave, **YOU ARE NOW SAVED!!!!** You will spend your eternity in heaven.

The next step is very important- you must find a Bible-based church that teaches the Word of God and confesses the Lord Jesus Christ to be the son of God. Don't delay. Do this immediately. Do not leave yourself open to the enemy. Get connected with the saints of the Most High God and keep yourself covered with the unspotted blood of the Lamb.

Here is my prayer for you.

Father God,

I thank you for the opportunity to minister your word to the unsaved, the unchurched, and the uncommitted. Father God, I pray now for the souls who have just received the gift of salvation. Lord Father, they have opened their hearts to you, and I know that you have received them into your kingdom and written their names in the Book of Life. Father God, I pray that you will touch their lives and show yourself mightily before them. Let their eyes be opened by the scales falling off, allowing them to see clearly.

Father God, I even pray for the backslider, those who have turned away from you after receiving the gift of salvation. You said in your Word that you desire that none would perish. So Lord, I send your Word to them right now, praying that they would confess the iniquity in their heart, repent, and turn from their evil ways, so that they may receive a life of abundance. You said in your Word in Matthew Chapter 14, that every knee shall bow before you and every tongue will confess that Jesus is Lord.

Father God, I pray now that we all come under subjection to your Word and that we will humbly submit our lives to you. I ask all these things in the name of my Lord and Savior Jesus Christ.

Amen, Amen, Amen!!!!

I will continue to pray for your success in your walk with God. Remember, this spiritual walk that you are about to embark on will not be an easy walk, but remember, the race is not given to the swift but to those who endure to the end.

Be blessed with heaven's best. I love you!

About the Author

Dr. Cassundra White-Elliott resides in California with her family, where as an English/Education professor, she teaches at various community colleges.

When writing, she composes with the direction of the Holy Spirit, in an effort to share with God's people all He has for them.

In addition to teaching and writing, Dr. Elliott also serves as an evangelistic teacher. She is also the founder of International Women's Commission, a ministry that serves the needs of the entire person, by attending to healing the mind, body, soul, and spirit.

Dr. Elliott holds a Ph.D. in Education, a Master's degree in English Composition, and a Bachelor's degree in Education.

Dr. Elliott is the founder and editor-in-chief for *Christian Inspiration* magazine, which covers topics germane to Christian living and the world at large.

Dr. Elliott is also the founder of CLF Publishing, LLC. For your publishing needs, go online to www.clfpublishing.org.

Other Works by the Author

(All books can be purchased at
creativemindsbookstore.com
amazon.com
barnesandnoble.com)

From Despair, through Determination, to Victory!

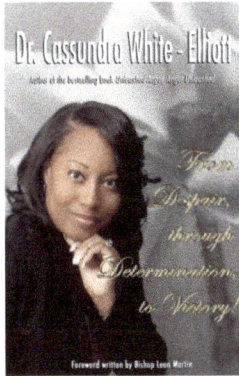

A lot can happen during a span of 40 years. The life of Dr. Cassundra White-Elliott has been anything but uneventful. From a fun-loving childhood sprinkled with incidents of abuse to a tumultuous young adulthood to a stable, secure adult life, she has experienced a full life, with much more to come. Her story is inspiring and motivating.

If anyone lacks hope, reading Dr. White-Elliott's autobiography will propel him/her into an attitude of "Maybe I can." This attitude, if nurtured and developed, will grow into an attitude of "Yes, I can." Throughout her life, Dr. White-Elliott has always held in her heart the belief that she could achieve anything that she had a made-up mind to embark upon. She was determined to achieve her heart's desires, doing what God has called her to do. She takes no credit for herself. All the glory goes to God, for He is her driving force. In Him, she lives, moves, and has her being.

Through the Storm

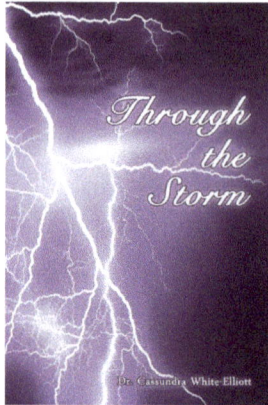

Through the Storm was duly inspired by the avaricious cloud of depression that decided to hover overhead of my daily existence in the latter part of 2007. Although I found it extremely difficult, I was once again compelled to not be defeated by just another snare that the enemy, the trickster, set for me. Once again, or more appropriately I should say *continuously*, he has exerted pernicious efforts to snatch the very life out of me by causing me to wallow in despair and to believe that I had been overcome by failure when in actuality and all reality, I was just experiencing a temporary setback. During those cloudy days, I had to remind myself daily that even though I was a target of the enemy, I am and will always be a child of the Most High God, Jehovah, who is my rock, my stability.

Unleashed Anger, Anger Unleashed

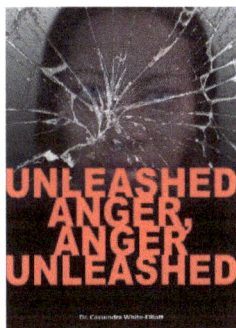

Introduction (snippet)

As I prepared to embark upon the adventure of writing this book, I had to prepare myself to also be transparent. I have found that being transparent is required in order for healing to transpire, healing for all those that peruse the pages of this book and myself. And I may as well tell you that today, at the onset of this project, I have not been totally delivered from my condition of being an anger-filled person. However, I am definitely a work in progress. I have made strides with the assistance of my Lord and Savior, Jesus Christ, who is the head of my life. Without his love, guidance, and teachings, I would not be the woman of God I am today. I shudder to think where I could be instead and will therefore not entertain the thought.

Public Speaking in the Spiritual Arena

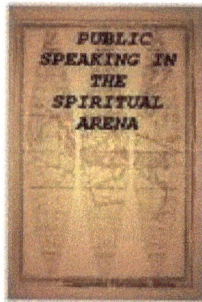

Chapter Two

How Communication Works

Purpose: This chapter will explain the six primary components of communication, identifying their purpose and how they work together.

The Source

In oral communication, the source of information is the speaker. In a church setting, the foundation of the message is God's word, but it is a speaker's interpretation of God's word that is delivered to the audience. As speakers vary, the information may vary but should have a similar essence because the foundational text is the same.

The Message

The message is the collective set of ideas that the speaker (the source) wants to deliver and/or illustrate to the audience. The message can be informative where the speaker informs the audience about a specific set of information. Or, the message may be persuasive in nature if the speaker wants to persuade the audience about conducting themselves in a specific manner, accepting God's commandments, or any number of things.

Where is Your Joppa?

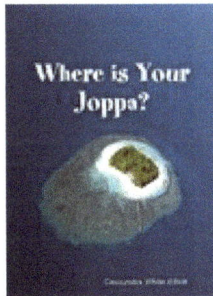

Where is Your Joppa? was written for the express purpose of illustrating God's call for obedience in the lives of believers with respect to the individual call that He has on each of our lives. As you read throughout the various chapters, notice that the emphasis is placed on our persistent disobedience in answering God's call in a specific area of our lives. We have become a people who are similar to the Israelites when they found themselves in the middle of the wilderness, following their exodus from Egypt. Before God, they murmured and complained about their current life conditions and failed to be obedient to God's statutes delivered through His servant Moses. Their persistent disobedience caused them to lose the opportunity to see and enter the Promised Land. I ask you, "What has your disobedience cost you?" "Was your disobedience worth what it cost you?" "Do you think about the souls you could have ushered into the kingdom of God?" These are some of the questions that I pray will be answered through your reading of the book.

Mayhem in the Hamptons

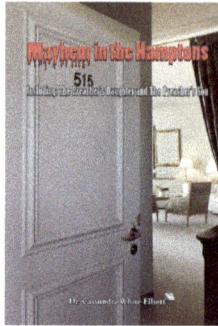

Romero and Yolanda optimistically plan for the day that is going to change their lives from being single persons to a couple who is united in holy matrimony. They, along with their parents, close friends and family, fly over to the infamous Hamptons, where only the rich and famous vacation, to have their dream wedding at the five-star Hampton Suites located on a peninsula in the Hamptons. Little do they know that their perfect day will turn out to be less than perfect when their wedding planner Mariesha Coleman suddenly goes missing!

A time when the newlyweds' lives should be filled with joy and the creation of wonderful memories, they are stricken with grief as they desperately try to find clues to help solve Mariesha's disappearance.

Mayhem in the Hamptons is a tale that shares how the horrors of a woman's past can come back to haunt her in more than one way and the impact it can have on anyone who gets in the way.

Preacher's Daughter

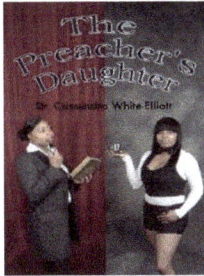

Tinisha, the daughter of a preacher, is a twenty-six-year-old God-fearing young woman endeavoring to complete law school so that she can make her mark in the courtroom. Working in one of the late-night clubs in Hollywood to earn money to pay her own way through school, Tinisha soon learns that life doesn't always go as planned. Finding her strength in her faith, Tinisha constantly finds herself praying as she watches God move miraculously in her life.

Preacher's Son

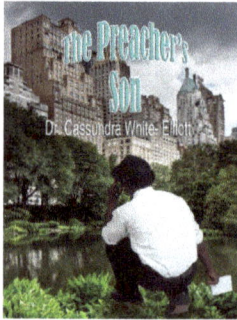

Romero Turner is a private investigator with a promising future. As he continues to build his career, he is excited about the cases he undertakes. However, his father Pastor Theodore Turner has other plans for his son's life. In the midst of trying to save his client's husband from Sylvester Domingo, a ruthless crime lord, Romero must try to salvage his relationship with his father. He must decide if ministry or life as a detective is in his future.

Lord, Teach Me to be a Blessing!

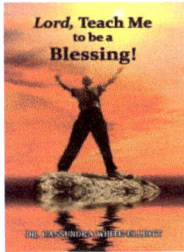

Lord, Teach Me to be a Blessing! will change a person's mentality from being centered around "me, myself, and I" to focusing on "others."

The world system teaches us that it is acceptable to place ourselves above others in an attempt to get ahead and even to survive. Herbert Spencer coined the phrase '*survival of the fittest*' after reading Charles Darwin's theory of evolution. This concept of surpassing and outdoing others is the world's philosophy.

However, the word of God does not subscribe to or promote this self-centered ideology, and therefore, neither should believers. We must hold fast to the truths outlined in Holy Scripture: "*Love thy neighbor as you love thyself*" (James 2:8) and "*It is more blessed to give than to receive*" (Acts 20:35).

While holding God's truths to be self-evident, we must demonstrate them to others, thereby showing them the way of the Lord of how to be a blessing to someone *rather* than looking to receive a blessing.

This is the very purpose of this book: to change the mentality of the world from being *self*-centered to *other* centered.

After the Dust Settles

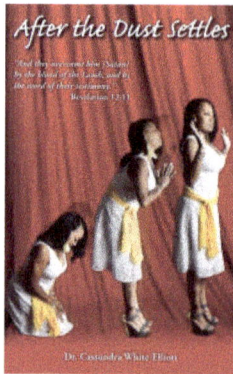

Throughout the journey of life, we all experience ups and downs and joys and pains. Most of us successfully find solutions to the situations/problems we encounter, but we often avoid dealing with the attached emotions. If we continue to ignore the emotions of pain, hurt, disappointment, anger, etc., we set ourselves up for destruction. Our families, our cultures, and our society tell us to be strong, to keep our chin up, and to grin and bear it. However, these methods of avoidance can lead us to strokes due to the undue amount of pressure we place on ourselves and/or mental illness from being unable to cope with the emotional baggage we have accumulated.

In *After the Dust Settles,* Dr. C. White-Elliott shares several situations that we all may encounter at one time or another in our lifetime and how to successfully navigate through them, so we can find ourselves emotionally healthy after the dust has settled and the situation has been rectified.

Begin reading today and experience a better tomorrow!

Claim Your Inheritance

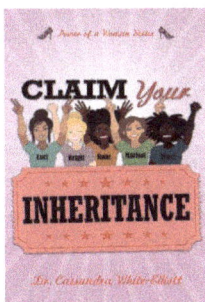

"The thief cometh not, but for to steal, and to kill, and to destroy: I am come that they might have life, and that they might have it more abundantly" (John 10:10).

Satan's mission is to steal, kill, and destroy all that God has provided for us. With him on the rampage, we must be ready to go to war- spiritually and naturally. On the other hand, we could sit idly by and allow the enemy to take what is rightfully ours. However, that is not the will of God. God has given us power to tread upon serpents and scorpions (Luke 10:19) and to reclaim all the enemy has stolen from us.

This book will share how we can be victorious in reclaiming what is rightfully ours when the enemy has turned his ugly head in our direction and made us prey for his latest scheme.

With God on our side, the enemy will not prevail!

A Diamond in the Rough

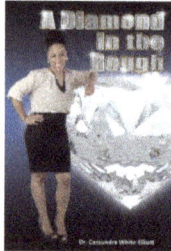

A Diamond in the Rough Architecture Firm was built and is owned and operated by lead architect Kyra Fraser. For the last five years, Kyra has been extremely successful in business, but her love life leaves much to be desired.

Kyra has set high standards for herself and does not wish to take a man in any condition and attempt to make him over. She is looking for someone who is drama free, well educated, very cultured, fun-loving, good looking, self-motivated, and the list goes on.

Will Kyra find the man of her dreams, or will her dream just continue to be a dream?

As you delve into this page-turning novel, Kyra's reality will unfold as you are drawn into her world of design, love and office drama- which includes her best friend's husband who is looking for love in all the wrong places.

365 Days of Encouragement

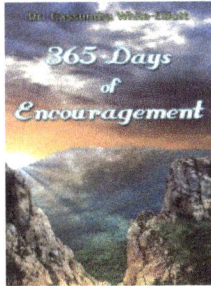

Just as our brain requires oxygen obtained from the air we breathe to sustain our mortal bodies, our spirit requires revitalization and encouragement in order to be strengthened each and every day of our lives. The revitalization and encouragement needed for the spirit of man comes directly from the word of God and assists us in walking according to the way of our heavenly Father. *365 Days of Encouragement* provides a scripture a day for each day of the year. Along with the daily scripture is a brief note of commentary also for the benefit of edifying the saints of God.

It is my prayer that the people of God would live a fulfilled life through Christ Jesus. Knowing His word and understanding we can walk in the fulfillment thereof is empowering. We are instructed in II Timothy 2:15, *"Study to shew thyself approved unto God, a workman that needeth not to be ashamed, rightly dividing the word of truth"* (KJV). Take an opportunity to delve further into the word of God, to know His statutes and to allow your own personal life to be edified, so you can be equipped to bring glory to God and lived a fulfilled life.

A Mother's Heart

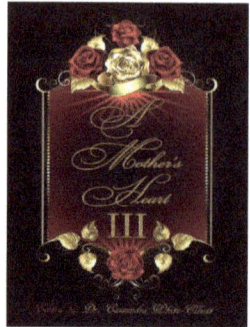

A Mother's Heart shares the unconditional love of mothers through a compilation of testimonies. Each testimony serves as a tribute to a special mother. The children of the represented mothers have lovingly written about their childhood, young adult life and/or older adult experiences they shared with their mother. As you read the writers' reflections, you will feel the expressions of love exude from the pages.

The purpose of this book is two-fold. First, it honors those mothers who stood by their children through the trials of life and showered them with unconditional love. Second, the book is a source of encouragement for mothers who may feel inadequate and question whether or not they are actually suited for motherhood. Our advice to mothers is, "Be encouraged; the journey of motherhood may seem daunting at times and you may shed some tears, but your children will never forget the love you have shown them and instilled in them to share with others."

Mothers may not be perfect, but they are definitely unmatched by any other category of person on God's green earth!

Broken Chains

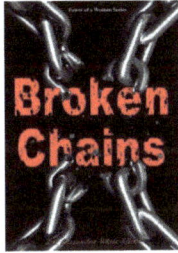

Broken Chains is an in-depth survey of five life-changing tragedies that can and will serve as chains to bind us if we are not watchful and mindful of their potential effects. In our lifetimes, we may all experience death of loved ones, sexual abuse, broken relationships, promiscuity, and sickness and disease. These everyday life occurrences can have detrimental effects on the remaining years of our lives and change our existence, unless we deal with them in a healthy manner.

Broken Chains not only brings to light the detrimental effects of five life-changing tragedies, but it also shares how anyone who experiences them can be healed and delivered from their effects.

If you have experienced death of a loved one, sexual abuse, a broken relationship, the effects of promiscuity, and/or sickness and disease and have not been able to rid yourself of the emotions attached to them or specific resulting behaviors, Broken Chains is for you.

God designed each of us for a purpose, and He has an intended end for us to achieve. In order for us to effectively achieve our God-given purpose, we must be free of chains that bind us. It is not God's desire that we become immobilized by life's events. His desire is for us to be healed, delivered and set free. Be healed today, in the name of the Lord Jesus Christ!

I Have Fallen

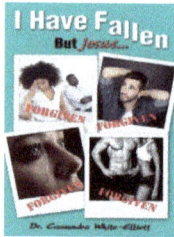

Do you know anyone who has committed his/her life to Christ but has done something unseemly that you would never expect a Christian to do? How did you feel about that person or what the person did? Did you pass judgment? What if that person were you? How would you feel if you made a misstep and no one forgave you and instead began to treat you differently? How do you feel when you are judged for past mistakes or lifestyles that are no longer part of your life?

This book shares four true stories of Christians who have made missteps during their walk with God. The purpose is not to air their dirty laundry, but to demonstrate our humanness and our vulnerability. None of us are exempt from making errors and falling into sin. It can happen to any of us.

The solution for these dilemmas is for the person who fell into sin to make a life-changing move and turn away from the sin, repent and ask God for forgiveness. His arms are waiting!

The next solution is for those who witness the sin or know of it. Pray and be of comfort to the one who has fallen. Lead him/her back to the path of righteousness. Love thy neighbor and treat him/her as you want to be treated!

The Bottom Line

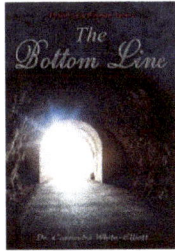

The Bottom Line is a detailed review of the Book of Job. Much can be said about Job's experiences with the loss of his children and wealth and the subsequent return of it all in mass proportions. However, the telling of Job's story in the Holy writ was not intended to focus on the return of his wealth. Instead, the focal point should be on the bottom line of the entire situation.

When you experience trials or tragedies in your life, do you tend to focus on the trial itself, the result, or the bottom line?

"What is the bottom line?" you may ask. The bottom line is the message God is sending regarding the situation.

When Job experienced his tragedies, there was a bottom line. Likewise, when you experience your trials and tragedies, there is a bottom line as well. It is up to you to discover it.

This book will reveal the bottom line in the Book of Job. It is readily apparent, but many often overlook it.

Now, it is up to you to uncover the bottom line of your experiences, for God will not bring a trial to you without a good reason.

Power of a Woman

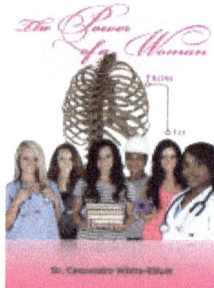

The ongoing conversation about the value of a woman is presented from a different perspective in ***The Power of a Woman***. Dr. Cassundra White-Elliott presents a biblical perspective of women and compares it to the worldview of both yesterday and today. This comparison seeks to illustrate God's intended purpose for His uniquely designed creation: woman. Dr. Elliott shares God's truth about pre-imposed limitations set by man versus the limitations God Himself set for woman in addition to the wealth of liberality He gave her.

Women's creativity and abilities are not meant to be stifled. They are meant to be utilized to bring glory to God, to help sustain and nurture their families, and to move the world forward. Knowing God's truth will show women how to celebrate and appreciate who they are as well as one another!

Women, let's take the blinders off, lift our heads up, and march forward, side by side with men, and bring glory and honor to God! Take your rightful place with a gentle smile and grace and be who God called you to be!

Every born-again believer has a God-given assignment. Whether or not the individual accepts the assignment is a personal decision. For those who choose to walk in God's will rather than their own must then follow God's divine plan for their life. Completing the God-given assignment means tuning one's ear to hear, receiving guidance, knowing when to commence, and, most importantly, exercising patience. Furthermore, the task may require enduring hardship along the way. A servant of the Lord can never fully anticipate what may occur during the journey of completing an assignment. What should be foremost in the individual's mind is completing the task, so he/she can hear the Master say, "Well done."

If you have never completed a God-given assignment, or if you are preparing to embark upon a new journey designed by the Lord, this book is for you. It will provide guidance for commencing and completing God-given tasks. If you feel intimidated by the task ahead, don't be dismayed. The Lord said He will never leave you or forsake you (Hebrews 13:5). Trust and believe that He will be with you every step of the way.

But you must act now!
Time is running out!

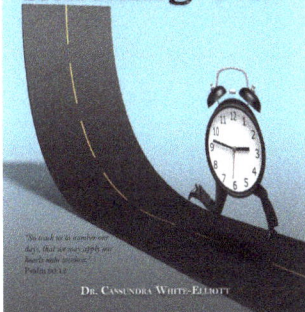

CLF Publishing, LLC.
www.clfpublishing.org

Dr. Cassundra White-Elliott's books are available at:
www.creativemindsbookstore.com
www.amazon.com
www.barnesandnoble.com

ISBN 978-1-945102-21-9

90000

9 781945 102219

Set Free

If you possess habits and display characteristics that are unbecoming, debilitating, and hinder the desired progress in your life or that affect your relationships with others, Set Free will provide the steps you need to be healed and delivered, through the Word of God.

Deliverance is available to you! Claim your healing today and walk in victory!

Do You Know God?

Have you or someone you know ever felt alone, confused, or unsure about your walk with God or are you unsure of what being a Christian is all about? *Do You Know God?* is an excellent text for providing answers to many of your questions. This book introduces adolescents and young adults to God in addition to answer many of their questions about being a Christian. This book shares the testimonies of the trials and tribulations that other teens have experienced and how God prevailed in their lives. All the information that is shared on the pages of the book is based upon the Word of God and the scriptures are taken from the King James Version of the Bible. If you are interested in knowing more about God's Word or how to begin your Christian experience, this book is for you.

Daughter, God Loves You!

"... for her price is far above rubies"
(Proverbs 31:10b)

Dr. Cassundra White-Elliott

Maybe you have heard the proclamation, "The world is going to hell in a hand basket!" Well, I believe I must concur.

However, I do *not* believe, we- the adult, mature believers- should sit idly by and allow our daughters (and our sons for that matter) to go with it! We must fight for our girls and young women, for they are the mothers of tomorrow, and some may even be young mothers today. Not only will they continue the human race, but also they can have bright futures in their careers and as leaders in our society, as they allow God to direct their paths and order their steps.

Daughter, God Loves You! is a n earnest attempt to address many of the issues that plague our society and turn our daughters' heads away from God.

In this book, we dive head first into topics such as God's love, the importance and impact of education, the effects of social media, overcoming abuse, and the proper perspective of the future.

For the young adult women- Reading this book will empower you to have a bright prosperous future from being enlightened about the dangers that plague our society and how to avoid pitfalls, as you walk along the path God has paved for you.

I invite all of you to take this journey with me to save our daughters and yourselves (young women) from corruption, by being empowered with knowledge.

We must thwart the plan of the enemy. So, LET'S GO!

CLF Publishing, LLC.
www.clfpublishing.org

Dr. C. White-Elliott's books are available at:
www.creativemindsbookstore.com
www.amazon.com
www.barnesandnoble.com

ISBN 978-0-9961971-9-9
90000
9 780996 197199

Web of Lies

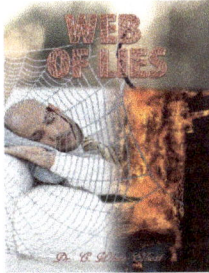

A year ago, Charlito Jimenez was found in his den, lying on the couch, with a fatal gunshot wound in his temple. Everyone in the community still wants to know who is guilty of the unfathomable crime.

Tinisha Salisbury, attorney at law, has taken the case of the accused. Can she prove her client's innocence or will a guilty verdict be rendered?

Halfway through the trial, a badly burned body was found at the scene of a fire.

Is there a string of murders being committed?

Are the murders related?

Web of Lies spins the tales of several characters into one web. Each has a story to tell, and everyone has something to hide. The web of lies, deceit, and revenge take over the lives of these characters to the point where they may not be able to see their way clear.

Embracing Womanhood

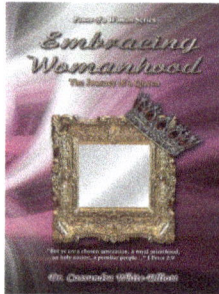

The journey from adolescence through puberty to young adulthood can be challenging and quite disconcerting for the average young lady. The changes that occur both mentally and physically can be both confusing and uncomfortable. However, the outcome of the changes can be beautiful. What she will experience during this time in her life is simply a metamorphosis – taking off the old and embracing the new. The process is similar to that of an awkward caterpillar that overtime develops into a beautiful, graceful butterfly.

The topics covered in this book (puberty, self-esteem, mental stability, goals, finances, and relationships) will assist young women (ages 15–23) in understanding the transformation they are enduring to prepare them for the life that lies ahead. After taking in the information, they will literally witness themselves evolve from princess to queen!

The Making of Dr. C.
A Memoir

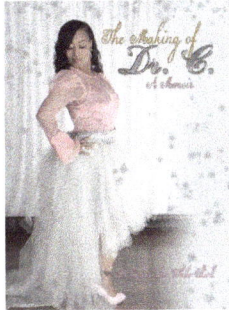

The Making of Dr. C. shares the 50-year journey of Dr. Cassundra White-Elliott. Her journey of trials, missteps, successes, and triumphs will inspire you to face any trial you may encounter with a positive attitude and the Word of God.

Her life demonstrates no matter what you may face, there is always a brighter tomorrow.

Keeping the faith will allow God to work in your life. After all, He only wants the best for you!

Prepare for Battle

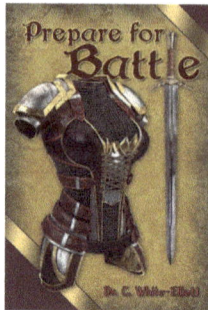

The very life you live is a war zone, riddled with battles ranging from the unexpected to the inconceivable to the paralyzing. The only way for you to successfully navigate through each battle unscathed or with minimal damage or loss is to equip yourself with the full armor of God, which consists of the girdle of truth, the breastplate of righteousness, the gospel of peace, the shield of faith, the helmet of salvation, and the sword of the spirit. To seal your victory, prayer is just as essential a component as each piece of armor. Therefore, the seven aforementioned items serve to comprise the arsenal necessary for winning wars.

This book goes to great lengths to explain each piece of armor in depth, with use of commentaries. The more you understand the importance of the arsenal, its function in battle, and how to effectively use it, the better prepared you will be when unexpected or inconceivable or paralyzing battles confront you.

Equipping yourself today for battle, with the full armor of God, will prevent Satan, our adversary, from annihilating you.

Safety in Him

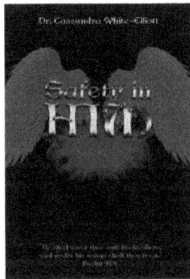

Luke 21:33 declares, *"Heaven and earth shall pass away: but my words shall not pass away,"* and Jeremiah 1:12 says, *"Then said the Lord unto me, Thou hast well seen: for I will hasten my word to perform it."* According to these two verses, we can stand firmly on the Word of God at all times because His Word is everlasting, and He watches over it continuously to perform it.

While the promises of man may go unfulfilled, God's Word is true and He declares, *"So shall my word be that goeth forth out of my mouth: it shall not return unto me void, but it shall accomplish that which I please, and it shall prosper in the thing whereto I sent it"* (Isaiah 55:11).

In this book, particular attention is brought to Psalm 91:1-7. In these verses, God promises His divine protection for His children. Read Christopher's story and see how the divine protective nature of God is demonstrated and remember Acts 10:34b, which states, *"God is no respecter of persons."* What He is able to do for one, He is able to do for another. So, no matter what you be faced with today, call on the Lord, and He will deliver you!

Women's Study Bible

NEW INTERNATIONAL VERSION

Red Letter Bible

CLF PUBLISHING, LLC

Learn the Bible Series

(26 books from A-Z to teach children biblical
principles and prominent characters.)
Currently available are A-R. More coming soon!

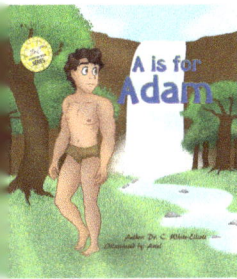

A is for Adam

B is for Babel

C is for Christ

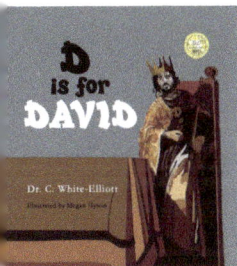

D is for DAVID

Dr. C. White-Elliott

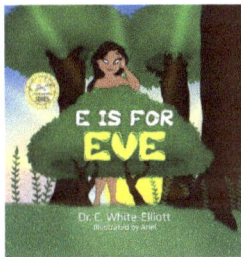

E IS FOR EVE

Dr. C. White-Elliott
Illustrated by Ariel

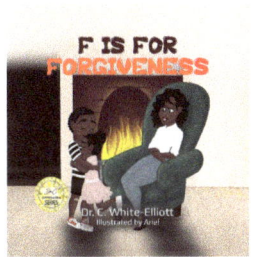

F IS FOR FORGIVENESS

Dr. C. White-Elliott
Illustrated by Ariel

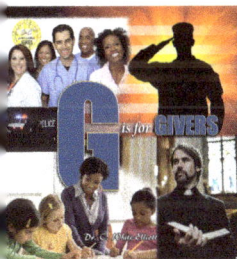

G is for GIVERS

Dr. C. White-Elliott

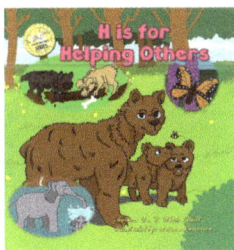

H is for Helping Others

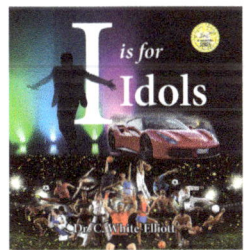

I is for Idols

Dr. C. White-Elliott

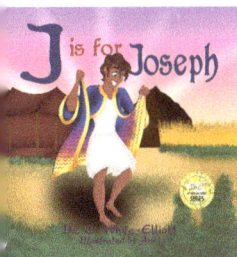

J is for Joseph

Elliott
Illustrated by Ariel

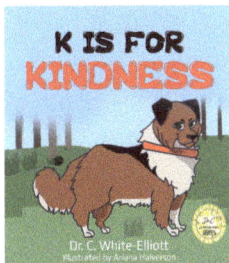

K IS FOR KINDNESS

Dr. C. White-Elliott
Illustrated by Ariana Halverson

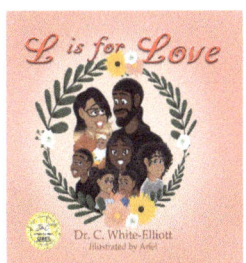

L is for Love

Dr. C. White-Elliott
Illustrated by Ariel

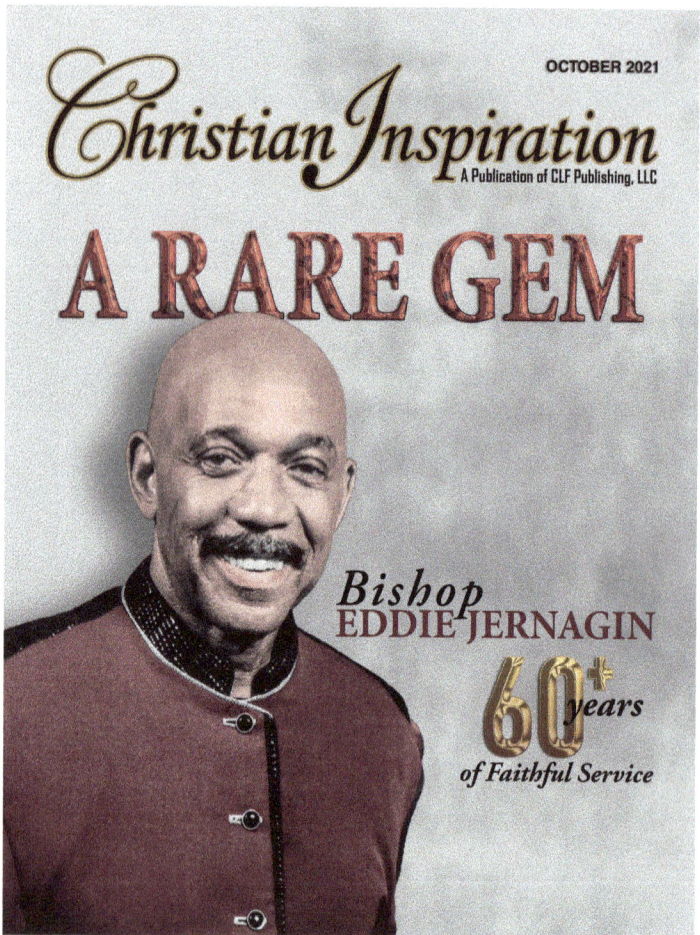

OCTOBER 2021

Christian Inspiration
A Publication of CLF Publishing, LLC

A RARE GEM

Bishop
EDDIE JERNAGIN

60+ years
of Faithful Service

Christian Inspiration is a quarterly magazine with issues released each year in January, April, July, and October. The magazine covers topics germane to Christian living and the world at large.

DR. CASSUNDRA WHITE-ELLIOTT

THE **LAST** SHALL BE **FIRST**

AN ANALYSIS OF THE SYSTEMIC SUBDIVIDE OF BLACK AMERICA

Beginning in the early 1500s, Africans were transported to America; however, they were not permitted to live and operate as free citizens in the new land. They were enslaved and treated as property rather than human beings. Some 500 years later, people of African descent and other Blacks have yet to realize the true meaning of freedom, equality, and liberty in America. This inequity stems from sustained and systemic racism and acts of discrimination. These abhorrent acts have consistently kept Black Americans marginalized from mainstream America, depriving them of equal access to employment, education, wealth, housing, quality health care, and safety.

The modern-day slavery experience of Africans in the 1500s and 1600s (which led to the current condition of Black Americans) was similar to that of the Israelites of the 15th century B.C. as they too were enslaved. At the moment of the Israelites' liberation from Egypt, God moved mightily in their lives by transferring the wealth (gold and silver) of Egypt to the Israelites.

In this season, God desires to move mightily in the lives of Black Americans as He did for the Israelites. And, just as He did for them, He wants to complete the wealth transfer that has already been initiated, for the Bible says in Proverbs 13:22b, "...and the wealth of the sinner is laid up for the just."

So, what must you do to prepare for a mighty move of God? How can you be an agent of change?

CLF Publishing, LLC.
www.clfpublishing.org

Dr. Cassundra White-Elliott's books are available at:
www.creativemindsbookstore.com
www.amazon.com
www.barnesandnoble.com

ISBN 978-1-945102-62-2
90000

9 781945 102622

Rest in HIM

Scriptures for Daily Peace

Dr. C. White-Elliott

Each day brings about its own unique challenges. Yet, in the midst of the challenge you are enduring, there are scriptures that are applicable to your situation that will provide insight, understanding, and comfort. God's Word serves as our guide and provides peace in the midst of a trial or daily circumstance. The Word of God keeps us healthy and whole when we read it, meditate on it, and apply it.

Rest in Him provides Bible verses at your fingertips for easy use. Keep this handy tool close by, so you can remind yourself that the Lord is an ever-present help in the time of need.

CLF Publishing, LLC.
www.clfpublishing.org

ISBN 978-1-945102-68-4
90000

9 781945 102684

www.ingramcontent.com/pod-product-compliance
Lightning Source LLC
Chambersburg PA
CBHW052129150426
42813CB00077B/2644